CAN YOU FIND MY LOVE? ™

On YOUR hEAD

JAN MARQUART

www.CanYouFindMyLove.com

ISBN: 0997330813
ISBN-13: 9780997330816

Cover and Interior by Publish Pros
www.publishpros.com

Books currently available in the "Can You Find My Love?" Series

Other Books by Jan Marquart

FOR ADULTS

Write to Heal

The Mindful Writer, Still the Mind, Free the Pen

The Basket Weaver, a Novel

Kate's Way, a Novel

Echoes from the Womb, a Book for Daughters

Voices from the Land

The Breath of Dawn, a Journey of Everyday Blessings

How to Write From Your Heart (booklet)

How to Write Your Own Memoir (booklet)

A Manual on How to Deal With a Bully in the Workplace

Cracked Open, a Book of Poems

A Writer's Wisdom

To:

_____

NAME

My appreciation to Rich Carnahan, who worked
tirelessly editing the details and photos for this book.
And to master Aiden, who gave valuable reactions to this book,
I send love and hugs. Thank you!

CAN YOU FIND MY LOVE?
is dedicated to all children.

May each child be filled
with love and the fun for learning.

You have received this book
because someone loves you.

Look closely—you will find love hidden
in everyday things that you might
normally take for granted.

This is what it looks like.

When you find the love I have placed
for you, I hope that it warms your
heart and lets you know how
very special you are.

You can put many things
on your HEAD.

ON YOUR HEAD

CHEF HAT

Chefs wear hats to absorb the sweat on their foreheads and to keep hair from falling into the food they are preparing.

CAN YOU FIND MY LOVE?

STRAW hAT

Farmers often wear cone hats made
of straw and wet them in summer
to keep their heads cool in the field.

CAN YOU FIND MY LOVE?

HEADBAND

Headbands started as bands
of leaves and flowers for athletes
who won games.

TOP HAT

Magicians sometimes wear a tall,
black top hat to hide the rabbit
they've stuffed inside it.

CAN YOU FIND MY LOVE?

BASEBALL CAP

Baseball players wear soft caps with long,
stiff bills on the front to block the sun
when they play ball.

hOODIE

Hoods, or hoodies, were
first worn by monks and people in
high positions of power.

CAN YOU FIND MY LOVE?

hARD hAT

Construction workers wear these helmets so they don't get hurt if something falls on their heads.

PARTY HAT

These fun cone hats show others
that the people wearing them
are celebrating a special occasion.

CAN YOU FIND MY LOVE?

SHOWER CAP

Some people wear these
plastic caps to keep their
hair dry when taking a shower.

CAN YOU FIND MY LOVE?

JESTER'S HAT

Fancy hats with bells on them were
worn by jesters to make kings and queens
laugh by looking and acting silly.

CAN YOU FIND MY LOVE?

GRADUATION CAP

A graduation cap, also called
a mortarboard, shows that you've
completed your level of schooling.

EAR MUFFS

Invented by a teenager, these furry circles strap over your head and cover your ears to keep them warm.

COWBOY hAT

The large rim protects cowboys
from rain, snow, wind and sleet
while shading their eyes.

CAN YOU FIND MY LOVE?

MOTORCYCLE hELMET

A motorcycle helmet's one purpose
is to protect the rider's brain if
he or she crashes.

PILOT'S HEADGEAR

The very first headgear for pilots
was designed to protect their eyes
and ears from wind and cold.

CAN YOU FIND MY LOVE?

BIKE HELMET

You wear a helmet when riding your bike to protect your head, and its reflective strips make it easy for drivers to see you.

CAN YOU FIND MY LOVE?

hEADPhONES

Headphones fit over your head
like ear muffs and are used
to listen to your favorite music.

SWIM CAP

Wearing a swimming cap
helps to keep water out of your ears
and your hair dry.

TIARA

Real princesses wear tiaras made of diamonds, but little girls wear tiaras made of plastic to look pretty—like a princess.

FOOTBALL HELMET

This hard plastic shell has thick padding inside and a wire mask on the front to protect your head and face.

CAN YOU FIND MY LOVE?

WIG

A wig is made of real or fake hair.
Change your hair to
change your whole look.

Did you look close enough
to find all my love?

❤️

Can you **DRAW** a few other things you wear **ON YOUR hEAD**?

Can you **DRAW** a few other things you wear **ON YOUR hEAD**?

Can you **DRAW** a few other things you wear **ON YOUR hEAD**?

From:

paste
photo
here

_____

NAME

About the Author

Jan Marquart is a psychotherapist and author. She has published 11 books for adults and has had articles, stories, poems and essays published in various newspapers, journals and magazines across the United States, Australia and Europe. She teaches writing for those over fifty and has taught a dozen writing workshops for Story Circle Network.

Jan has designed a 6-week writing course titled *Unveil the Wounded Self - Write to Heal* which focuses on healing PTSD and has also designed a 6-week writing course titled *The Provocation of Journal Writing* to encourage everyone to write their personal stories. She has written over 100 daily journals.

Jan can be contacted at JanMarquart.com, JanMarquartlcsw.wordpress.com and at her personal email address, jan@canyoufindmylove.com.

Her books can be purchased from all major online book retailers.

www.ingramcontent.com/pod-product-compliance
Lightning Source LLC
Chambersburg PA
CBHW040248100426
42811CB00011B/1190